THE UNBELIEVABLE ADVENTURES OF GABBY & JOSH CAN ™

JOSH'S CLAM-TASTIC SPENDING QUEST

STORY BY
LATASHA WADDY

IMAGERY BY
SOPHISTICATED PRESS

ISBN 979-8-9921467-0-7

Follow the adventures of the Can Family and learn more about the author and the series at:

hello@latashawaddy.com

@latashawaddy

Publisher: LECO HOLDINGS, LLC

Imagery

&

Publisher Consultant

"Sweet dreams, son." Mamma says, kissing my forehead.
I giggle as she tickles me while she tucks me into bed.
She knows too many thoughts are swimming in my head!

SPACE
EXPLORING

Daddy will take me out tomorrow to spend my bucks.
We'll have guy time, and I will buy a sand truck.
"I can't wait!" I declare, "I can't count sheep."
Mamma laughs, "I know, but you must get some sleep."

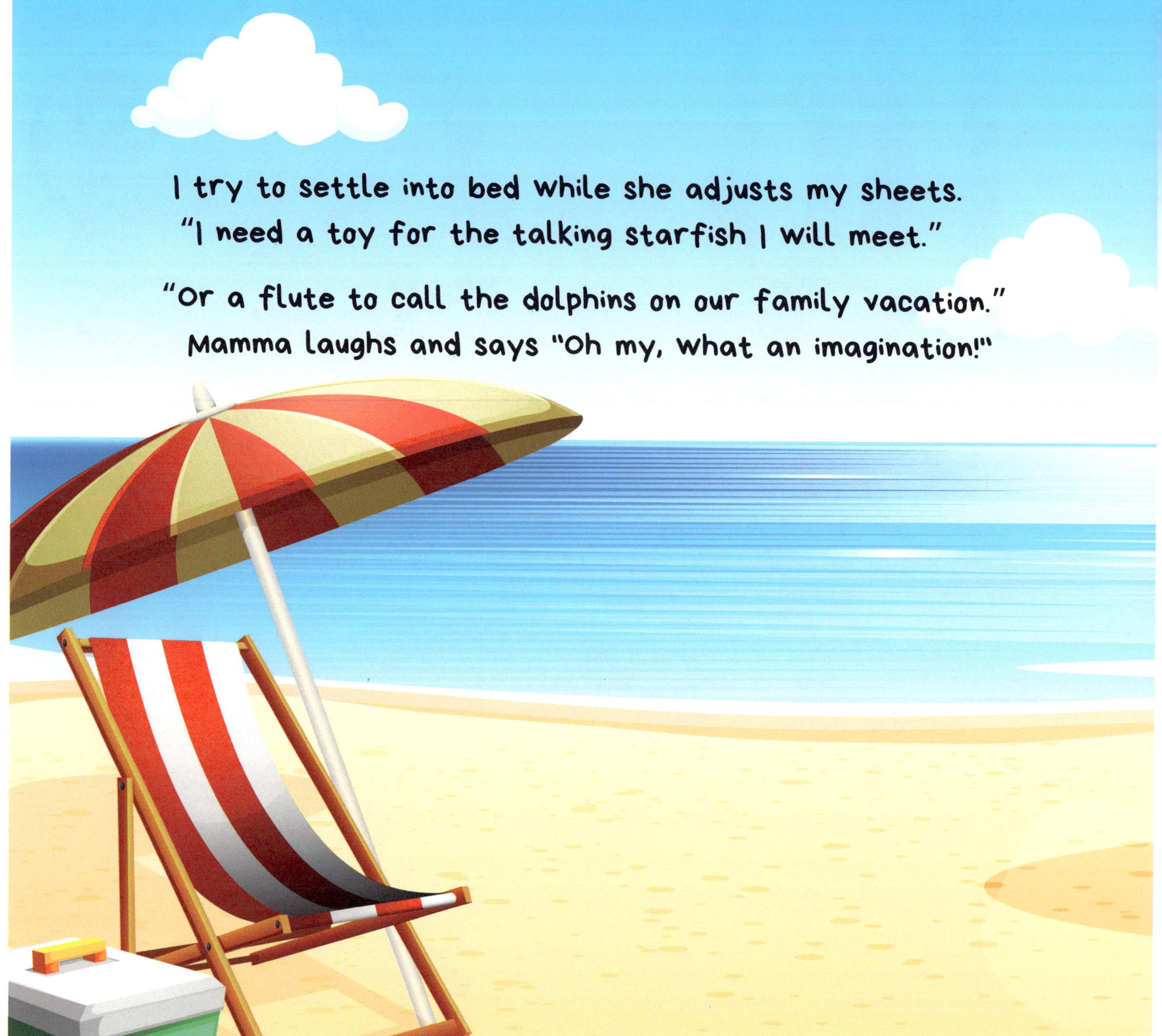

I try to settle into bed while she adjusts my sheets.
"I need a toy for the talking starfish I will meet."

"Or a flute to call the dolphins on our family vacation."
Mamma laughs and says "Oh my, what an imagination!"

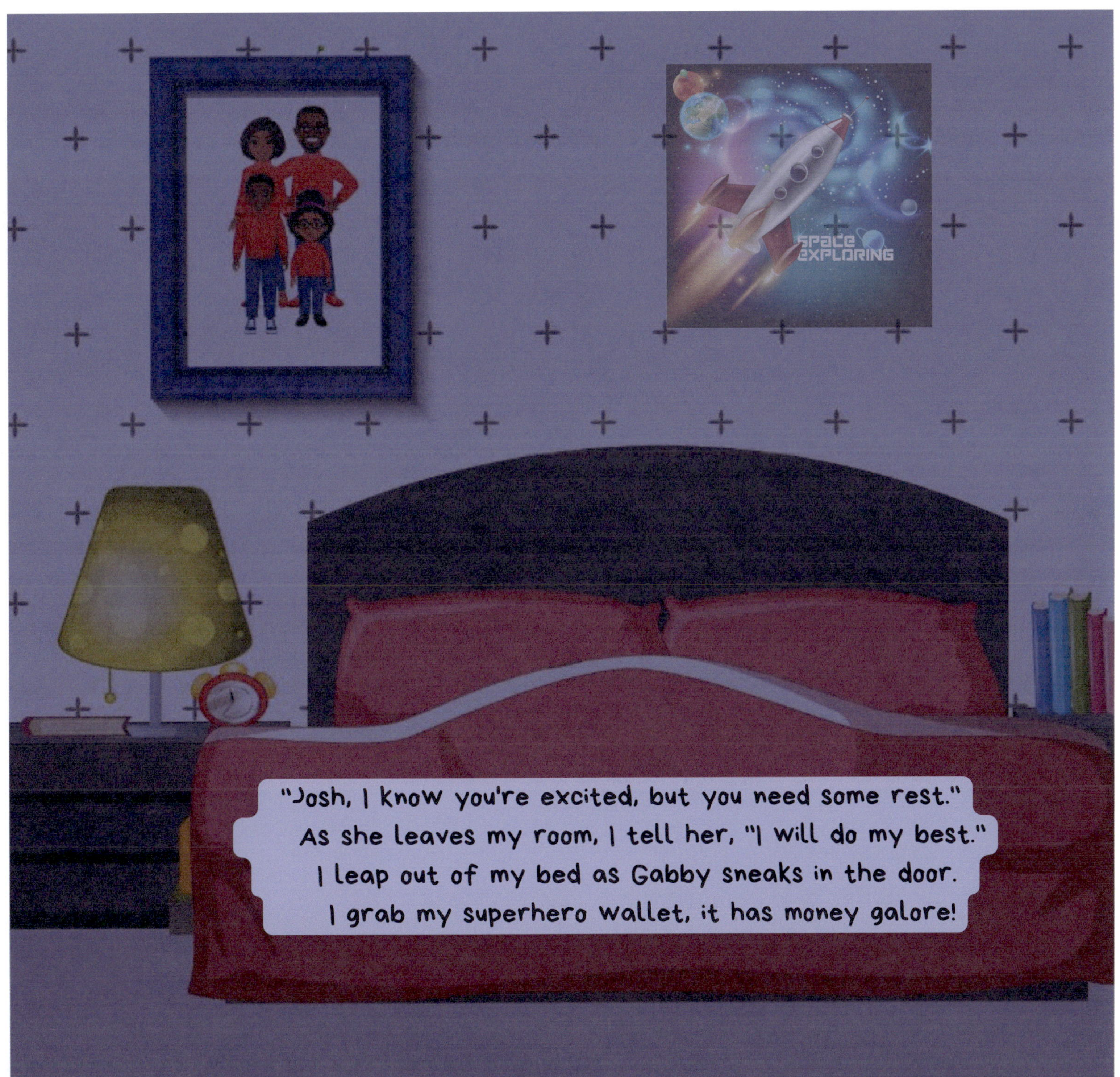

"Josh, I know you're excited, but you need some rest."
As she leaves my room, I tell her, "I will do my best."
I leap out of my bed as Gabby sneaks in the door.
I grab my superhero wallet, it has money galore!

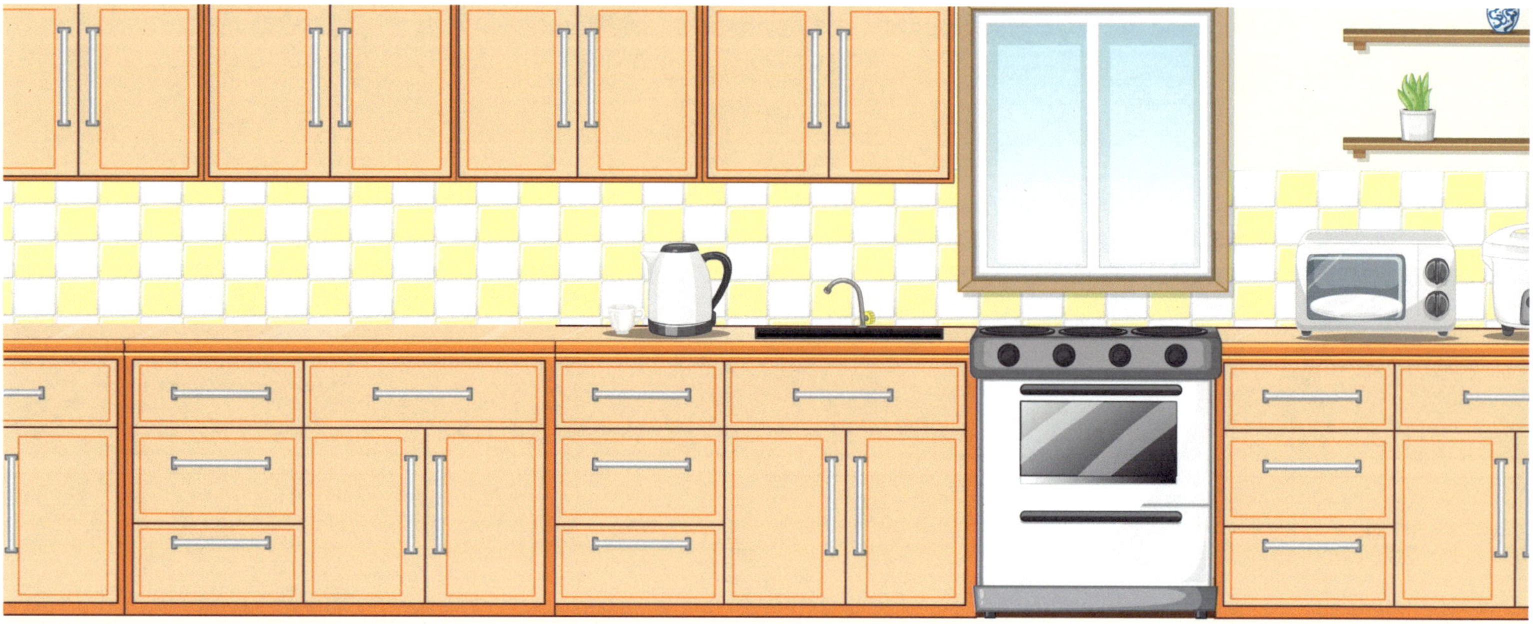

By doing chores, I earned money to spend on our trip to the ocean.
I hope Daddy doesn't make me buy something boring, like suntan lotion.

Reuse Me

I count my earnings, feeling quite proud.
"I have 35 dollars and 65 cents." I say out loud.
I try to keep it down, since it's still night.
"Spend, spend, spend!" I whisper with delight.

I tell Gabby I will buy her a toy that blows bubbles.
We hurry back to bed before we're in trouble!

SPACE
EXPLORING

I close my eyes and soon I am surprised.
I find myself underwater with sparkling blue skies.
Instead of my room, I'm surrounded by the sea.
Everything is enchanting and feels so free.

Daddy swims towards me with a big smile.
With our new sea gear, we can stay for a while.
"Son, we use dollars to spend on dry land."
"But underwater 1 clam is like $1 dollar." I nod yes, I understand.

He hands me 5 big clams to spend on something fun.
"Let's visit the Sea Superstore, our adventure's just begun!"

SEA
SUPERSTORE

The sandcastle store is where sea people shop.
There are so many things to buy and the clams just don't stop.

I find a shiny red dump truck that costs 5 clams.
Daddy asks "Is spending all your money your game plan?"
He points to a shovel that costs 1 clam and a pail that costs 2.
"If you save some clams, you can buy something later too."

I think about what Daddy has to say.
I agree, "I might need these clams for another day."
But what would I do with a shovel and pail?
I can't spend all day collecting seashells!

I decide that the truck is more fun for a beach day.
Daddy says, "Ok champ, let's get in line to pay."

As we leave, we hear a very loud sound.
The items in the store are flying all around.
I cover my eyes as Daddy says, "Hold my hand."
I think to myself, this never happens when we shop on dry land!

When I open them, I'm back in my bed, and everything's dry.
My superhero wallet is next to me, and I let out a sigh.
I'm happy to be back home, but I wonder how it could be.
Just moments ago, I was spending clams in the sea.

KNOCK
KNOCK

There's a knock at the door and I hear a voice I know.
It's Daddy asking, "Hey champ, are you ready to go?"
I tell him about our underwater adventure and the clams we spent.
How it is ok to spend, but not every cent.

Daddy hugs me and asks, "Josh, what else did you learn?"
I say, "It's important to save some money, not spend all that I've earned."

SPACE
EXPLORING

I get dressed and decide that I will spend $15 today.
"I can save for another time and put the rest away."

SPACE
EXPLORING

I now know money can be used in many ways.
To enjoy the present and save for future days.
Today, I learned that earning money is just the start.
Making a plan to spend and save money is smart!
100

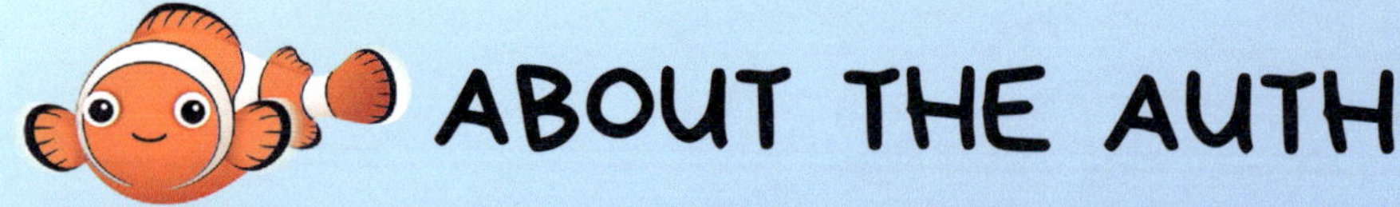

ABOUT THE AUTHOR

LaTasha Waddy is a dynamic finance attorney, children's author, and speaker dedicated to empowering young minds through education and creativity. Josh's sea escape is part of the 3-part series "The Unbelievable Adventures of Gabby and Josh Can". The series introduces foundational financial literacy concepts to children ages 5-8 through fun, engaging storytelling. Her mission is to equip families with the tools to spark meaningful money conversations, helping children develop healthy financial habits early in life.

LaTasha has four beautiful children and is also a third-generation homeowner, having purchased her first home at the age of 25. With over 20 years of experience in the financial services space, her passion for teaching the next generation about finances was reignited during the pandemic when she, like many, balanced working and caring for her children. This experience fueled her desire to help parents normalize conversations about the often, taboo topic of finances.

Through her experience, LaTasha uncovered three key questions that inspire her work:

1. When did you first learn about finances?
2. How did your childhood shape your relationship with finances?
3. What do you wish you'd learned earlier in life about finances?

These insights were the catalyst for the creation of "The Unbelievable Adventures of Gabby and Josh Can" series, designed to excite young readers and their families to build a solid foundation in financial literacy.

When she's not writing, LaTasha enjoys spending time with her family, traveling, and discovering new books to add to her book library.

Made in the USA
Columbia, SC
02 May 2025